Sanctified

Sanctified

An Anthology of Poetry by LGBT Christians

Edited by Justin R. Cannon

Sanctified: An Anthology of Poetry By LGBT Christians
Edited by Justin R. Cannon

ISBN: 978-1438247854
First Edition.
www.sanctifiedanthology.com

ACKNOWLEDGEMENTS

I would like to thank my parents, Nancy and Richard Cannon, for their help with editing this anthology and for supporting me in all my countless "projects". I want to thank Christopher Dombrowski for bearing with me as I obsessed about the cover, and for his love and support. Lastly, I want to thank *everyone* who submitted a poem to this anthology. I received many excellent submissions, and unfortunately could not publish them all. It was hard having to send out notices to those poets whose works were not selected for publication. I hope you all keep writing and know that your work is beautiful whether it is published or not. Keep on dreaming. Keep on praying. Keep on writing...

NOTICE TO THE READER

Censorship quite frequently limits the creative process. Because of this, none of the poems in this anthology have been censored for any reason. They may contain adult language and mature themes unsuitable for children or adults offended by such content.

ABOUT THE EDITOR

THE REV. JUSTIN R. CANNON is the founding director of Inclusive Orthodoxy (InclusiveOrthodoxy.org), an affirming outreach ministry to lesbian, gay, bisexual and trans Christians centered on his study *The Bible, Christianity, & Homosexuality*.

Fr. Cannon graduated from Earlham College where he received his B.A. in French and Francophone Studies. During his studies at Earlham College, he served on the editorial board for *The Earlham Literary Magazine* and started up the school's poetry appreciation group, Poetheads Anonymous.

He was ordained to the priesthood by the Right Reverend Marc Handley Andrus, Bishop of the Episcopal Diocese of California, on December 3, 2011. He lives in California with his two rabbits, Perpetua and Felicity.

TABLE OF CONTENTS

THE POEMS

STEPHEN BARTLETT-RE

Untitled Poem

Once
children were
sacrificed to placate
the gods for a time
but more was required
more sacrifices, more
costly offerings to quench
the gods' greediness

God sent His Son
who sacrificed himself
once
and all humankind
was reunited to God
once for all

But the urge to control
God still controlled humans
who demanded their children
sacrifice themselves for
their parents' greediness
all for nought
once again.

STEPHEN BARTLETT-RE

Christmas 2003

The garlands gently sway
    across bomb-blasted window frames
in hopes of business for the stalls in front
    in back the dimness shrouds the mother
holding her first born
    a glowing miracle of beauty
calling forth both love and awe
    God's gift to all who see

In muddy alleys children throw
    loose stones at strangers who
invade their playground then
    lie shot by men the age
of brothers lost but yesterday

Today who can afford to love
    yet God still offers all to bear
replacing hearts locked shut
    with broken breathing hearts
perhaps to mend into a new
    and unexpected wholeness

JEFFREY BARNES

Irene

She had dreams too
And insecurities
Then she became a wife
And a mother
And a mother
And a mother
And a mother
Then mine
Those others they were
Making the way for me
Preparing her for me
That's not true
      I'm selfish
She's mine mine mine mine mine
She had a shell
She broke out
I think she is resting again
      In the broken halves
I want her to stand up
Stomp the shell
      Grind it into the ground
Sing - sing loud
Sing pretty
Revel in her beauty
She is beautiful
She really is
I want her to know that
      -believe that
Look in the mirror
Look inside
      -deep inside
see the beautiful woman
accomplish her dreams
feel worthy
worthy to be Irene

JEFFREY BARNES

Raisin Gran

Red Kitchen table trimmed in chrome
Linoleum floor pretending to be stone
Raisin bran for two is what she pours
Flakes ping and clank into clear glass bowls
We share a special moment
                    A raisin or two from the heap
                              Before milk drowns all
Perfectly round spoons dive into crunchy sweet goodness
This precious ritual I now relive as I
Plunge my spoon into crunchy sweet goodness once more
                              Into the same sacred bowl

BEN BARTON

The Row

Coarse phrases of endearment,
perhaps – or deep-cutting insults

dredged from murky fountains
of wisdom. Every word you throw

at me, you chip, chip
Chip away another fragment, another

piece of me comes crashing
to the floor, until one day

Soon, you will have smoothed
me out. I'll be stood there

as still as Mrs Lot
pale alabaster.

A stalactite.

BEN BARTON

Commandment No.5

My father is a stranger to me
He never turns-up uninvited
Sitting cautiously on the sofa
Genteel
He waits – never asks
for a mug of tea.

My father hasn't always been
This stranger in my life
We were close, once
He organized my life, an official referee
Strict

He holds my gaze, unsure
if he loves me…

J. MICHAEL BRAIDEN

Crazy Quilt Bride

People hunting
for snakes that tell lies.
Accusing lambs of being wolves,
requiring tribal like loyalty to ideals
they construct borders and erect walls.
Who can know the TRUTH
when it's a crazy quilt gown
worn by a bride whose face is a frown.

J. MICHAEL BRAIDEN

Resurrected

You are unapproachable;
shrouded by mystery
and misinformation.
You are terrible and terrific!
The gates of both
Heaven and Hell
await Your command.
Blindness strikes us by day
and terror by night
for we are not upright
if those who measure and weigh
judging who we are
what we do
and every word we say
are to be trusted.
They are the self-appointed
centurions at the gate
the protectors of the faith
who purge the church of all
who are unworthy and unclean.
The gates have closed us out.
But we've been out before.
We are the outcasts,
infidels
and heretics of faith.

(continued on next page)

We are unclean
un-circumcised
and unworthy too.
We are eunuchs and lepers
unwanted by most
though we've been filled
with the Holy ghost.
Slain by the law,
resurrected by Grace.
In spite of it all
we are the ones haunted
by the memory
of Your face.

J. MICHAEL BRAIDEN

New Cloths

The elusive truth
runs out of view
escaping capture
circles back
and sneaks up on you.
Pulling the rug
from under your feet
tearing down walls
yanking down order
like proper drawers.
Just when you think
the cement has dried
and all the rules
are true and tried
and they know we are
Christians
by those we exclude.
God starts laughing
He knows
the Bishop is nude.

J. MICHAEL BRAIDEN

04/05/06

It is not the idea
of love that appeals
to me.
The object of love has captured
my affection. Friendship is the
best beginning. From there
we travel the winding paths that weave
through Agape, Phileo, and Storge,
arriving at Eros. More than a
destination: a compound
as when hydrogen and
oxygen correctly combined
become water.
We create something new and different:
A third thing.

J. MICHAEL BRAIDEN

Polite Society 1

I've only seen Jacaranda
In the city,
never in nature.
Domesticated flora, an
upside down
exclamation point
releasing its flowers
on the breeze like
purple confetti tossed on
New Years Eve.
Manicured to the point of
obscenity, nearly perfectly
round
unlike in nature
where chaos and
randomness reign and life
unabashedly thrives
unencumbered by
polite society.

J. MICHAEL BRAIDEN

Alchemy
(What Mother Taught Me)

When I was young (Yes
very young)I was often
teased (with out
mercy). "You are sooo
weird." "You throw
like a girl." "Are
you a transvestite-
? I think you are."
Weird is the word
that hurt most
by far. I feared
it exposed some fatal
flaw; that I had trans-
gressed some universal
law. Or worse (That I might
be different) One
day Mother (I will never
forget this) sat me down and
said: "When someone calls
you weird thank them, it's a
compliment." I believed
her (and I still
do) When someone (continued on next page)

calls me weird, to this
day, I always say "Thank
You."

J. MICHAEL BRAIDEN

Irrepressible

1) I'll take my cue
from the trees. Though
cut down they are
still unstoppable, growing
back with a vengeance in a
flurry of wispy green that
seems to say "Ha- Ha, you
can't stop me!" They keep on
growing; new shoots springing
from seemingly dead trunks.
2) Even Sidewalks,
blankets of cement, are not
heavy enough to keep a tree
down, when Buckled and broken by
unruly roots. Trees are
irrepressible.

NATHAN I. BRISBY

(For Matthew Shepard)

I think about the way the sun hit your face the day they killed you
And whether it blinded you so you couldn't see their evil.

I think about what your future envisions:
To see your partner grow old, and your young son – now a man.

And I wonder if the last thing you thought was
Whether redemption and warfare were synonyms?
Maybe you laughed as you thought about Christ's resurrection
And, in the end, His victory over death.
Maybe you listed the people you could
Honestly say you loved.

Maybe you thought about what it would be like:
If there were gold streets and crystal seas,
And love everlasting.

And I'm sure you thought about the finality of it all.
I'm sure you knew this country would be much the same
before your death as after.
Not much would change.
It would mostly be the same.
Mostly.

Except for a young man who would
Be reborn.
And this time,
He would think about truth and loving kindness
Rather than revenge or restraint.
A young man who would continue to ask what you thought
In your last day when the sun hit your face
A man who curls his brow, picks up his pen and mantras,
Death be not proud

NATHAN I. BRISBY

Apprentice

How many times did He clap two pieces of wood
One against the other for a hinge or a chair
And see visions as he nailed one to the other

He looked into the desert and saw the north wind
Blowing toward the highlands, dust in the air
And remembered how he was born of the wind – dust and breath

He thinks what heavenly creature makes the sun turn into night
And the sky open up with eternal fire
And for how long does it last
If it was his forbidden punishment to wear like rain

NATHAN I. BRISBY

8-10-04

I wanna write a poem about how it sucks to be me

I wanna write a big, long fucking poem about how it sucks to be me.

But I can't seem to concentrate on things sucking when I look around me and I write a poem on my laptop, I am boarding a plane to visit parents who love me (despite myself), I have enough money to buy the occasional starbucks chai tea latte, and my piss is not red from blood vessels bursting in my urethra (or Aretha...no, that's the queen of soul).

I wanna write a poem about how life can suck when your gay and Christian and you came out of the closet as a gay man FAR before you came out of the closet as a Christian who loves Jesus Christ. But, that poem is self-indulgent and unprofound.

I wanna write a poem about being 25 (almost 26) and proposing that I live at home for another two months while my friends nearly cry wanting me back so badly.

I wanna write a poem about hurt, and pain, and anger (I am fucking mad), and a poem about being white and middle class, and how it has afforded me little priveledge. But, then I realize that is a pack of bold-faced lies. I walk into stores and don't get accused often of stealing, I get smiles instead of fear from strangers, and police officers don't assume I'm a druggie wanna-be-rapper who beats his wife and does illegal acts daily.

I wanna write that kind of poem. But, instead I will write this:

I am profoundly grateful for the blessings of a God who loves all of me : dirt and all.

JUSTIN CANNON

Across Eternity

For Christopher

I do not know if there are words in my vocabulary
That can comfort you in your despair or sorrow or doubt or confusion;
All I know is that those are places that I too have and do and will inhabit.
In the darkness of pain I do not know
If you or I can touch each other's wounds in life-giving ways
Or if we can be ushers of joy, carrying light for each other into those
  spaces.
I do not know if I have the strength to support you when all your
  emotions collapse
And you are suspended above all the questions and insecurities of life.
I cannot pretend to have answers to the questions that hold you close to
  the earth
And reflect your frailty and even my own.
I cannot breathe life into your mouth as I too am gasping for breath
Afraid of fainting and falling deeper into the spacelessness of feeling.
There is but one thing I can do for you and you for me.
In this dark space, though we may not have the vision to guide one
  another,
I can hold you close and you me so we know we are not alone,
Collapsed in each other's arms,
Punctuating each other's unanswered questions,
And laying together close to the earth—
Gasping side-by-side for hope,
Holding each other's heart not as a doctor or surgeon,
But as one reminding the other that these feelings, even numbness,
  witness that we are alive.
And at the end of the day, I can only speak three soft words to you—
Not because you can comfort me or I you,
Not because you can breathe light into the shadows of my life—
But because some still small voice assures me that I am not alone—
And something leads me to believe that that is your soul whispering
  across eternity to mine.

JOHN COONS

Fill

Blowing thought bubbles from my ears,
They drift and burst on the hardwood floor,
Leaving behind only soapy footprints,
Emptying me from the top down,
Hollowing me out like a Chocolate Easter Bunny.
I drain myself like the tide,
Only scattered seaweed memories and shells of old pains
Left on the intestinal beach.

Ready.
Ready for you to fill me up
My cup runneth over
With thick black ink
And white birch smoke
Until I cry your stars
And bleed your dreams
And when I open my mouth to sing,
your song is the sea
Rushing in to reclaim its kingdom
as we fall to the deep.

Like the petrified forest
The two timbers of my legs
Are slowly worked away,
Pushed out of themselves
Until only a mineral facsimile is left,
A fossil of me made only of you.

Fill me.
Fill me with your smile
And your pain
And your scars
And tears and jokes and nightmares and invisible childhood friends,
Until my pores clog with fiery bronze,

(continued on next page)

And with a single crack on the skull,
I halve myself,
Revealed to be only the mold,
Not the statue.

Fill me as a lover fills his daydreams,
As heartbreak fills a poet's quill,
As warmth fills the space between the bed and the blanket.

Until I float in myself
And my eyes close to hold you in
Like they hold in my dreams when asleep,
Until there is no room for alone
Or afraid.

Until I can't breathe
Because even the wind can't
Pass through the space between
Our intertwined fingers.

Until the atoms themselves
Dance around us,
Searching for a crack
Like a mime's hands on his invisible wall.

Until even time takes a detour,
Turned aside by the inseparable
And the cosmos hinge and pivot on our souls.

JOHN COONS

Blankets And Cathedrals

Nice bed,
Does it come without straps?

You know the kind I'm looking for-
Not too small, not too big,
Comfortable,
Doesn't enslave you to your dreams so you can't get out of bed for fear
of losing them to the world?

Hah, I know what you're going to say,
"This from the guy that walked into church and said, 'Nice religion- do
you have one with half the guilt?'"

But seriously, I'm just trying to be an informed consumer, be it with my
bed or my faith.

I mean, there are some things you just have to know about your religion:

How many miles to the gallon can you get on the sacramental wine?
How did Consumer Reports rank your congregational contentment?
Is this whole church Made in the USA or just the fundamentalist parts?
Does it come with a No Purgatory Guarantee?

But, anyways, back to the bed:

What's the dreams to nightmares ratio on this queen size?
Is this bed eligible for the optional Pillow talk add-on?
With the current ratings of my love life, is getting anything bigger than a
twin bed too optimistic?

Don't you hate those people that buy a bed for all the wrong reasons?

Will this bed make my penis look bigger?

Well, it was either this or a TV, and I think that the bed would be more entertaining.
Now, this bed comes with a super-absorbent pillow for my excessive moping, right?

and don't get me started on those pseudo-Christians!

Quick question, the membership entails that I just LEARN the Beatitudes, not LIVE them, right?
I bought this model because of the gets parents off my back package!
My church? Oh, I love it! It runs completely off of holier-than-thou!
It feels great to fit in with all the neighbors. I mean, after Nancy got one, I practically HAD to.

I guess that I'm not surprised that we've consumerized our religions or sleeping surfaces. I just hope that I get to see their faces,
When the beds that have room for sex but not for love break down and they're forced to look in a mirror. .
When their running-on-fumes faux-faiths peter out, and they're forced to actually think about the nature of God.

Me?

Give me a bed to support my back and my heart
And a religion to support my knees and my soul.

It's all about finding the difference between supported and being held down in the end anyway.

So, yeah... nice bed,
do you have what I'm looking for?

JOHN COONS

The Crayola Crusade

The first time I saw a gray brick,
I knew precisely what I had to do.

My pudgy five year old fingers
plunged
into the crayon box,
rooting for a red
and were determined to set things right.

Nothing was ever broken... it was just colored the wrong way.

I didn't blame God for my new crusade,
my quest to BRICK RED conquer the concrete,
to GRASS GREEN govern the wheat fields,
to BARK BROWN bully the birches,
to SKY BLUE subdue the rainy days,

Clearly, to my superior five year intellect,
He had just forgotten.

Armed with cannons of Crayola,
I knew that the world would soon be
Picture book perfect.

Of course, it came as quite a shock
when I found out
He had not adorned me with
the popular palette.

How I longed to be colored
IN CROWD PERIWINKLE
or DUMB JOCK APRICOT
or DATING THE CHEERLEADER LAVENDER

(continued on next page)

instead of
GEEK MAUVE
AWKWARD NEON GREEN
and OH SO LONELY BLUE.

But the worst,
the most painful discovery
was when I discovered
that God had colored my heart
the wrong way.

You see, with all the
ROMAN CATHOLIC MAROON
and
SPARKLING FAMILY VALUES WHITE,
there was no room,

none,

for HOMOSEXUAL PEA SOUP GREEN.

Wrapped in wax garments,
I colored myself,
covered myself,
in 8-COLOR masks
and Yellow Cardboard Box Armor-
and my tears were
BITTER AZURE
and
GOD BLAMING TURQUOISE.

I was surrounded by nonbrown birches
greenless wheat
cloudy skies
and anchored within,
a heavy Gray Brick
in the pit
of my stomach.

(continued on next page)

My last thought scribbled away in my mind
as I hit the gritty pavement,
and the box slipped from my fingers
and scattered around me in a halo of spear shaped shades,

"If only I had a
                    single
        red
                            crayon."

SHARON E. CUTTS

Chapter Of You
(fire in the house)

My friend, full of life, so strong and clear;
I admired your strength and gentleness,
your connection with kids.

You saw me in ways that you hid for years,
but it began to show and you confessed your fears
that telling would cause the friendship to cease;

So much to consider, yet you found peace
in our platonic bond that deepened with time.
How could I say what had begun to stir?
That meeting your eyes seemed new and deep,
and should not be there.

I questioned these sparks, they had no name.
They spoke not to my head, straight to my soul they came.

These sparks were sharp and soft and rare.
My interest had deepened and now I would share
 your fears of destroying lives that had been
 built over years.

I had to tell, the sparks wouldn't stop.
They came to visit again and again.
They sat down right next to the platonic pair.
They cajoled me to speak that which shouldn't be there.

Your eyes widened, your thoughts seemed to race.
The sparks came again—they had found their place.
Like a fire in the woods, meant to clean out the brush
meant to show other ways,
meant to bring new life.

(continued on next page)

The decision has come, the fire has passed.
Embers still burn, much didn't last.

Through the ashes smoke rises, from black to gray,
Where's the new life?
Could there be a way?
Then clear as could be, deep, tiny and pure, rose wildflowers
in the heat of the ashes that stirred.

There are seeds that will only open with the heat of fire,
You are my seed.
I am your desire.

TREY DAYTON

North

Under the drift
of frozen stars,
a scarred and regal world
reposes, eyes half-closed;

white hair braids around peaks,
knotting with dark water,
sending cold ribbons into the ocean;

barren, flutes echo into silence
through the parted lips of the earth;

glaciers' glassy eyes gaze blankly;
dust disturbed upon the tundra-
raising its head to see
its own turbulence against tranquility;

pale fingers, lazy,
drifting, stroke
black velvet seas;

rhythmic, slow breaths, swelling-
receding; swelling-
receding.

EDWARD GERARD DEBONIS

True Believer

My sister stands
at the foot of our Father's bed
as though she is looking at Jesus
just down from the cross.
Presiding behind an altar,
a maestro, a shaman.
She lifts His sheet
its full width
like a magician
guiding it like a
linen veil,
it flutters,
covers Him.

Beneath the cloths,
she truly believes
a miracle will happen,
a re-orchestration of
chemicals, never before heard,
a white dove on the
end of her hand,
blood from wine,
flesh from bread,
his strapping athletic body
resurrected
from the ravaged remains
that cannot walk.

EDWARD GERARD DEBONIS

The Way You Dance

We don't dance
at straight weddings
because I won't.
And when everyone forms
a circle, dancing in place
and couple by couple
takes center stage
grinding each other,
you say: "Come on".
But I won't.
You look so
disappointed.
I can throw an arm
over your
shoulder and even
kiss you on the
cheek when no one's
looking our way.
I don't care if they see.
But when confronted with
a dance floor
a line from my
head to my heart
sends out chemicals
of self-hate
crippling me
and I know
I have so far
to go before
I learn to dance
the way you
dance.

EDWARD GERARD DEBONIS

Everything's Different Now

Everything's different now.
The whole world is chemically
changed since Mom is gone.
Dad is literally disintegrating
before our eyes.
I'm in shock, walking
through air as thick as
molten lava.
Mouthing words
that seem cynical and uncaring
as they escape.
Trying not to talk about Dad
as though he's not here.
Whispering about Mom
because Dad remembers her
sometimes. He holds hands
with a vice grip of steel
digging his nails
into my hands
either hanging on
to the end of his life
telling me
"Don't let go of me"
yet. Or using all his strength
to say "Let me go".

CHRISTOPHER ALAN GASKINS

When I Write, God Rises

When I write, God rises; He's nodding His head.
He has waited so long, His Heaven a hill and with Him upon it,
for me, like Milton, to impart what I've said
both hither and thither, give birth to a sonnet.
"Leave your love in a rhyme, it is that they'll remember,
your faith inside metaphor. I have given you this gift."
Even now, in depression and half through December,
I draft single-handedly; the other one is stiff.
But belief becomes language to color intent,
every poem is breathing, slides out from each finger
and falls on the page. It resolves what I meant.
Sullen effort recedes. Unencumbered, I linger
over words I would worship while untying the ends
under God, who has waited; we are making amends.

CHRISTOPHER ALAN GASKINS

The Company I Keep

I get high on Sundays,
waiting
for God to come visit, for His image to fall in
right through the ceiling or
knock at the window.

"Come in," I smile, too stoned
to stand.

I offer Him Kool-Aid and nowhere to sit.
"No couch. No chairs."
But I'm saving my money. So, then
we sit
on the floor
and I show Him my poems.
We listen to Enya.
Leaning together, I pet unknowingly a swimming of tingles
inside of my skin, slipping a hand
underneath my shirt
and against the ribcage. I read
over His shoulder, as quiet as any
meek student of submission -
a smile, a sudden
lowering of eyelids, a dismantled
tongue
that I hide in my pocket. Like
this,

I watch Him turning each page, nuzzle my
unshaven chin
close against His nape,
harvest
lint from His sleeve, breathe
                    downward

(continued on next page)

a belief
built poem by poem
line up all my apologies and embarrassed disclaimers
as words in patterns take turn
in order
and hit upon air. But God doesn't give

any sidelong glances, no lilt
of the lip.
He knows already

every lyric-bound rape, a past full of fists
and psycho-analysis,
gay libido, my
father,
my usage of hate as a trial and error, the hairline fractured
jerry-built heart, this
sadness
eroding all leaflets of life in my black
3-ring notebook.
He forgives me my stupor, high
as I am.

He makes no comment, ignores the
joint
hanging limp in my fingers. He nods His head
and then He is finished.
He sits in silence. The music ends. My glass of Kool-Aid
is empty.

But God doesn't leave,
so much as He backs out of view whenever I am turning
around or unblinking. He goes
at last,
having heard what I've martyred in line
                                    after
                                            line
of repetitive rhymes,
through diction gripped as the numbness
ebbs

(continued on next page)

and for that I admit Him, become
as One
and put out the joint.

MARIO GERADA

Rhythms Of Understanding

Native to my own soul
feeling human
at the sight
of the rising moon.

Life seems so void
in our everyday chores,
so rich and meaningful
when confined.

Betrayed,
by beliefs and expectations
of happiness and love.

Accepting,
pain and loneliness
as a natural process of this life.

Gratefulness,
knowing we did nothing to be alive,
knowing we did nothing to acquire
the ability to breathe
the ability to move an arm
the ability to see,
to hear.

It's all a precious gift.

Standing,
at opposite sides.

Seeing,
the ugliness and beauty
of each side.

(continued on next page)

Understanding,
we are not alive,
we need to come to life.

Deprived,
of that which we mostly need.

Giving,
out of which we don't have.

Sinning,
understanding the life
of the Saints.

Wisdom,
living the other way round.

Discriminating,
between what's human
what's Divine.

MARIO GERADA

The Monk

Lonely footsteps
of a youthful monk
echoing through the silent corridors
of an ancient monastery.
His robe
trailing in the dust
of antique wisdom
and novel thoughts.

Marked earth
by the monk's feet,
walking amongst
the clenching need
of a love felt
on one's own skin
and not only in spirit.

Walking amidst
the wisdom of the mind
the desire of the heart
the cravings of the body
the longing of the spirit
the divinity of the soul.

MARIO GONZALEZ

You, *Fiend*

Then there is you
You exist as a malevolent medley
Administering vials of sins seven deadly
Yet another species of malignant scum
In the bowels of putrid hatred sprung from
Skewring hearts to set on rotisserie afire
Devouring troughs of faithless souls entire
They father, a darkly fallen angel to abhor
So too art thou ignorance
Thine enemies prayed for
Longing to toss you in a vat of His blood
Be cleansed!
In which for mercy you shall wade with His
Zeal condensed

So you,
Who bringeth fear and inflict pain
To dwell in delight and hazard betwixt,
Shall soon thy salvation
Through *Christ Jesus* be fixed!

MARIO GONZALEZ

Erosion

I always leave a piece of myself wherever I travel far
I'll pluck a hair from my head and blow
it out the car
Looking up at a different sky I
see the same star

If I'm on a beach in a foreign land
I'll leave a drop of my blood in the sand
In a different ocean with the same
water I stand

Every time I go to a far away place
I feel like scraping a scab off my face
Scattering around my blueprinted lace
Marking a trail throughout the day
To offer as my solemn homage to pay

When I feel too privileged to
be where I'm at
I leave something behind in a
place where I sat
Peeling from my callused hands a
piece of dead skin
I lay it to rest in this place
I'd never been

Because I take back with me so much more
A gratuity for a place I never
visited before

When I come home I like knowing that a piece of me is still there
I'll start planning my next trip if there's still enough of me to share
To continue practicing this customary ritual
And return eroded into a better
residual
A more detailed version of me the individual

HEIDI GRIEPP

The Cocoon between what crawls and what flies

(from the title of a Thomas Merton Journal Entry)

I refuse to go back to crawling.
I am terrified of being seen flying.
So I live in a cocoon, a holding environment.
The cocoon between what crawls and what flies.

And when I feel it coming off, I pull it back around me.
And when people tell me how to fly, and where to fly,
Or that I can't fly forward, or should fly backward.
I go still, and pull the cocoon around me.

And then I rumble and grrrrr.
Angry, still, glaring at the world.
Because they keep me from flying
But do they? And I get even stiller and pull the cocoon around me.

But the damn thing won't stay on!
My wings are fully developed
I am bigger than the cocoon can hold
I have to face the vulnerability and judgment of the sky.

No. I'm not ready, I don't want to.
But cocoons are not meant to be forever
And there are too many living-dead already
In cocoons between what crawls and what flies

So I'll snuggle in one more day and maybe tomorrow
I'll think about, thinking about, leaving
the cocoon between what crawls and what flies.

HEIDI GRIEPP

Virginity

My virginity is NOT a thing to fix, concur, lose.
Damn-it. It just is.
My virginity, is NOT pen-ultimate, like the church says
with it's years of paranoia, making sex into more and less than it deserves.
And to "you know who you are" ms. indiana
My virginity needs no help, just contextualization.
So you rule makers and rule breakers
You who call at me from books and steeples
From dates emails and you match-up peoples.
STEP OFF!

CHAD GURLEY

Dear Leonardo

what can i say now?
what do i tell you
now that you aren't here?
what does this world
look like, really?
who really
understands my tears?

questions.
and you said
we should live them.
but you stopped.
and i don't know what
to do with that.
i'm lonely.
i'm broken.
i'm searching.
i'm afraid.
my faith is shaken
to its core.
and i don't know
what to do with that.
i'm lost.
i'm in great pain.

you were my best friend.
my best friend.
i know people don't say that
after the fourth grade,
still
you were my best friend.
My only brother.
My always.
The one who got me.

(continued on next page)

That one person on this Earth
who really gets me.
Understood the words
coming out of my mouth
whether quiet or loud.

We whispered about
our cosmic connection,
that fateful day
the subway doors slid open;
my destiny finding
you waiting for me there
and we knew we would
always be together.
i thought we would,
always be together.
Leonardo and Chad.

Oh my Leonardo!
My Soulmate.
My One.
Who i missed out on.

Within my personal
confessional,
i would say
that the resounding
answered 'why?'
must be
that i wasn't there
for you.
i allowed
my own suffering
and depression
to drown me
so much so
that I missed
your call.
and you missed
my call.

(continued on next page)

and we missed
calls
all the way
around.
Damn!
i let you down.

please please
forgive me.

so now missed calls
are replaced
with missing you
missing our magical
Peter Pan companionship,
playing together
as adult children
all these ten years
we shared
in our twenties
and just a little
beyond.

in life
you did
inspire me
so much:

to understand and embrace:
the fun of climbing trees
and trekking along wooded trails.
the humor of our innate silliness
in making funny faces, clownish gestures,
and speaking in cartoonish voices.
the freedom of somersaults and handstands
in the crowded sheep's meadow
no matter who was watching.
the ecstacy of movement,
expressing feeling through dance.
the confidence of staring

(continued on next page)

across a room towards another
reaching for your eyes.
the great importance of accepting
a loving touch.
the creativity in drawing
outside the lines of convention
and tradition.
the silent disruption
of wearing torn disealed jeans
while conferencing with
suits of the republic of bananas.
the necessity of standing
up for ourselves,
debating those
who say we are wrong.
the sheer and utter joy
of wearing dresses without any shame.
the fulfillment in my finally
accepting the girl in me.

i felt us grow together
as you nourished a new me
away from the timid, self-hating
little boy you first met.
i grew
in your learning me to express myself
as an individual.
i grew
as you taught me to accept
exactly what i am feeling,
without the shoulds or should nots.
i grew
as you showed me that anger
is a worthy emotion
to be embraced and used for good.
i grew
as you broke down those walls within myself,
silencing the harsh voices
who said i shouldn't be.
i grew

(continued on next page)

because you demonstrated to me
that we can be,
we have dignity,
so i have the right to be me.
i grew
because you gave me
the courage to live.

and now you've died.
and i don't know what
to do with that.
i'm confused.
i'm hopeless.
i'm abandoned.
i'm angry
because i feel
like you cheated me,
that you cheated you.
everything i learned from you
i guess you were still learning too.
but there was so much more
growing we had left to do.
Yet you were ready to end your dance.
through playing with chance.
the time was up,
the pain too great to bear,
the tears exhausted,
so you made your exit.
and that makes sad
so very, very sad,
so that i don't know what
to do anymore.
i'm stagnant.
i'm empty.

for i love you so much.
you must know
that i love you.
you must know,
i love you so much.
did you doubt it? (continued on next page)

did you believe
that you were not
loved?
did you think
i wouldn't notice
your absence?
did you forget
my eternal love
for you?

well if you remember,
then meet me again
someday,
back in fourth grade,
my best friend,
i'll wait out
on baseball's right field
sitting in the grass
picking at clover
for no one is hitting
out here
except maybe you
and we will talk
and talk
and listen
and listen
and talk
and listen
and then
we'll laugh
just before becoming silent
at your finding
our four leaf clover,
then we'll escape together
over the hedge
long before
the game is over.
next time.

i will miss you so much
until the next time.

CHAD GURLEY

To Cry

i feel as if i might
burst into tears
at any moment.
walking down
the sidewalk,
eyes glazed,
staring off ahead
of me at a blur.
i notice only
the streaks of light
twirling around
the fluorescents
in a kind of dance
of melancholy.
and it seems
always this way.
and it seems that
this is the way
i feel the most comfort,
yet the most discontent.
i hardly remember
what love felt
like anymore.
i can barely remember the joy
of looking into a face
who looked back adoringly.
and yet,
i am not even sure he's
who i am missing or sad for.
i feel that i
have broken
my own heart
somehow.
inadvertently,

(continued on next page)

i smashed it
with my own unkind words
and scolding.
it's as if i must
abuse grace
to believe it,
or strive for perfection
in ignoring it.
i teeter from one side
to another
unable to find balance.
and this petrifies me
into a place
of complete
and utter
stillness.
i do not
move.
i stand
alone.
and it
is
there
that
i
begin
to cry.

CHAD GURLEY

Gutter Times

i've fallen back down into the gutter
and still i hear echoed footsteps stop
Light beams through the bars' shadows
and His hand reaches through lines
to touch mine

LINDA HEIDENREICH

I Wannabe Like Jesus

I wannabe like Jesus
in the temple with a whip,
turning tables
on homophobes selling
the souls of their children for
so many pieces of silver

'cause if David really l-o-v-ed Jonathan
and -
John did lay his head
on the breast of
the Good Shepherd

then surely Jesus loves the little homos
or at least is in touch with
"the little gay man in all of us."

LINDA HEIDENREICH

Broken (A Queer Catholic Perspective)

In the dark of morning
pray the morning prayer
Oh my God, I offer you
all my thoughts, words and actions,
and sufferings…

I offer you Harold
who died of AIDS and indifference
AIDS and profit
in a hospital
in a bed
two doors down from treatment.

I offer you Gwen
who died of indifference
and four male friends who
beat their manhood of out her
then went to McDonalds for breakfast.

And somewhere in the mix of it-
In the mix of it
we are Christ
We Are Christ
We have become the Great Sacrifice.

LUCAS ROBERTO HOARE

Calvario

Where shall eternity find me?
To be quite literal and faithful to the church
My only final abode is in the final damnation of all souls

Why is this the case?
For who and what I am to be acted out is gross sin,
That I know this fact and continue on my way is sin mortally so.

Why then am I unrepentant?
I am a curios child of God, one who has ever quested,
Yet for my "sin" due cause for its harm I have failed to find.

Am I thus calling others to my path?
Others would suppose this of me, but it is a treacherous way I walk
The way but a hair breadth thick and on either side a most ruinous fall.

What then are my motivations and cause?
To love and to be loved, to be nothing but that which God asks of me
Not for any gain other than pleasing my lord, my god, my savior.

If by my own self serving rational I fail to see and grasp a true order of
his,
And my due punishment be eternal suffering despite everything else that
I am.
Then may my damnation fall swift and heavily for He is God and I am,
Nothing but limited and imperfect man.

LUCAS ROBERTO HOARE

God's Passion for Those of The Cut Sleeves

Oh how God doth love us of sheared silk!
We are among those of the promised land of honey and milk.
We are among all places and all peoples.

We are not miscreations of a perfect being.
Neither a colossus or a basilisk nor a hippocampus
Lies amongst the least of us.

We doth shed blood, sweat and tears ,
For every reason that any other would.
Our hearts, minds bodies and souls all cast from one mould.

Yet you would have us all of cut sleeves be one and the same.
When like you we are both the same and nothing alike,
All at once, a truth despite your dislike.

For if you would think that god would hate us,
Solely on the basis that our union bring not a sapling forth,
I say that your God and ours is not one and the same.

For doth God not judge us on the basis of who we are,
The very nature of our hearts and minds, not
Upon how literally our actions mirror Cannon.

(continued on next page)

In cannon I can place little trust other that what my heart

And mind can both discern as high and true.

For in mindless obedience evil doth lay its deepest root.

God's inspired word you haughtily proclaim!

And therein lies my motivation for careful reasoning,

God may have inspired, but it is man who put his words in writing.

Lest we forget the many things forged in Our Savior's name.

Crusades, Jihads and mutiny stimulated by truths twisted and turned,

So that the real truth and the "enemy" both lay interned.

Be careful of the arrogance you cultivate!

For though it is a fact you are loathe, to admit and see

There are amongst, even us, a number far saintlier than you pretend to be.

And it is those that I would say to you

If God doth condemn to the greatest and never-ending agony

Based upon that single solitary aspect of their personality.

Then I truly fail to comprehend the least bit of our Lord!

For how can one who teaches to treasure and nourish love

Destroy even a single soul for that and nothing more.

LUCAS ROBERTO HOARE

Perdido (Lost)

Ya no me reconozco
I don't even recognize myself

E caminado por camino que nunca hubiera antes
I've walked paths I never would have before

Y ido a larguras que tanto evite
And gone to lengths I so avoided.

El camino esta pasando tan rapido
The road is passing by so fast.

Ya ni puedo decir adonde estoy.
I can't even say where I am.

Su caja de Pandora parece que abri
Pandora's Box it seems I've opened.

Adonde antes estaba segura ahora es arena movediza
Where once was secure is now quicksand.

Donde esta el nino que era?
Where is the child I was?

(continued on next page)

Donde esta el hombre que quise ser?

Where is the man I wanted to be?

Puede ser que estoy llendo muy rapido para que puedan seguir?

Can it be I'm going too fast for them to follow?

Las cosas estan estusiasmados!

Things are hyped-up!

Las cosas estan divertidos!

Things are fun!

Pero siento un vacío oscuro.

But I'm sensing a vacuous dark.

Un hoyo fantasma que comiera mis partes mas brillantes.

A phantom hole that would consume my most brilliant parts.

No quiero eso necesito a Dios!

I don't want that I need God!

Hace mucho tiempo que e hablado de veras con el.

It's been a long time since I've really talked with him.

El agarro mi mano para tanto tiempo.

He held my hand for so much time.

(continued on next page)

Ahora el hijo prodigal aprece que me e convertido en.
Now it seems the prodigal son I've become.

Mi Corazon esta pesado y mi conciencia esta cargado.
My heart is heavy and my conscience is loaded.

Lo que necesito es tiempo.
What I need is time.

No tiempo para fiestas.
Not time for parties.

No tiempo para.
Not time for.

Tiempo para centrarme otra vez
Time to center myself once more.

Tiempo para equilibra las cosas.
Time to balance things.

Tiempo para buscar el camino en vez de andar perdido.
Time to find the way instead of wandering lost.

LUCAS ROBERTO HOARE

To An Overshadowed Soul

Your Nights are cold and slumberless
You wish you could be more than emotionless
Inside beneath the permafrost of bitter years
A heart so tender and raw so far and so near

But the past is ever present
Every joy tainted by the formless beast
The hurts that will not mend, the memories that never fade
All around they permeate every action until nothing is left but regrets

At best life seems an opportunity to help other with their cares
though you've no desire for it yourself.
And the fears. the nameless fears of unanswered questions and eternal
doubts,
that you shall never outrun that cesspool and in your agonies your soul
shall drown.

You cannot fathom why you let love escape
Why you cannot let go and give trust.
But I tell you this, trust that you have all your answers
Trust that those you have not will come in time when they are due

And know that I love you and am one of many
For the greatest love is not only of lover's spent
but of a heart that understands your fears.
A love different but love nonetheless.   (continued on next page)

I have my own answers that I have found but cannot share

for part of the wisdom is to know that these are medicines only if self realized.

For therein lies the greatest paradox

The final fight and mend are yours to commence and conclude

whatever strength I and others have to give your reserves and not the cure.

LUCAS ROBERTO HOARE

Why?

Why do I care so much when all it does is hurt?

Why do I push everyone away when it only amplifies the pain?

Why do I care for your lack of love and care?

Was it not I who bid you good riddance and paid the fare?

Why do I yearn so much for company when I want to be left alone?

Why am I always the last to be informed and never the confidant?

Why am I plagued with these uncertainties?

About my love and desires that are so wrong,

To every fiber of truth and morality I hold dear.

My ideals which set me so far apart, when all I want is to be near,

Yet I must keep for sanity and integrity's sake.

My stony silence when my heart is dying to burst forth.

Oh why can't anyone see my pain and misery?

Oh why won't you be the one to break these iron chains?

These binding pains,

formed by the breaking of an innocence and naivety,

Once possessed an age and a half ago,

lost far before its time had come.

Why?

I know the answer all too well.

Too broad is the smile that masks my shattered soul.

(continued on next page)

Too quick my anger bulwark of my offense from hurt.

Too thin my defenses,

No more than paper against a shower of stones,

Easily repaired yet allowing every one to pierce my broken heart.

RYAN HOLLIST

4 A.M. Madness

A kind of madness comes at 4 A.M.
When all I can do is watch TV,
listen to the furnace fight the cold,
and let my mind wander free.

Phrases come freely, unedited and pure.
I have the words to tell of facing death,
of when I knew true love,
of when the divine touched me.

But I do not have the strength to put pen to paper.
I can only listen for a time, then sleep,
waking to a rested sanity,
and the words are gone

TIMOTHY HOLYOAKE

The Thief

Early summer flowers bore witness
     to the simplicity of youth that day.
A train cut through the green hills
     like a finger tracing a scar.
Sis and I made games with no rules
     as the daffodils stood guard to our play.

My name was called and I did go
     to the door I knew so well,
and the promise of ice cream
     to cool the heat of our summer swell.
Severing the bright beam of sunlight,
     he closes the door behind me,
to reveal the familiar dark room
     both around and inside me.
"Sit over there and I'll give you what you want."
     Touching my bare knee – *'How are you today?'*
I stare at the glow of the Holy water font.

Large fingers awkwardly battle
     with the little buttons on my fly.
Plastic belts bind my hands to a chair
     I can't move, I can't move, "It's ok, good boy"
The feel of leather smarting the skin of my back

(continued on next page)

seems to suspend sweet oblivion for a later day.
My crying goes unheard and my voice too betrays me
for it like my mind, has slipped away.

My hands are free as he brings my reward,
I run to the door, fingers touching the screen.
My shorts at my ankles impinge me,
I fall to the floor,
"Don't you want your ice cream?"
"Come back, sit down, stay.
Sssh with the crying, a big boy like yourself.
Whatever would people say?"

I run like I have never learned to walk,
Get up, get out, get through the door.
My sister playing alone looks up in wonder,
I don't stop to her tears as she sees my blood pour.
In the arms of mother and the scent of her comfort
I stammer and stutter and scream.
"There, there, its ok, you're a good boy."
She coos with the promise of ice cream.

I still run and as I do, can only imagine the day,
for it will come, when as a man I will revisit
the darkness of that bright summer day.

TIMOTHY HOLYOAKE

Sole To Soul

You haven't stepped in dog shit,
as your face seems to declare.
I can tell the sole of your shoe is quite clean,
for I can see it clearly from here.
Yet you look at me that way,
as you pass me by.
A disgrace you say, a sore in the public eye.

You don't know my name,
but you know where to find me.
I could tell you why I sit upon the street,
a shadow of the life I left behind me,

Now hungry, weak and always tried,
I am ever so slightly broken.
But you'll never know if I'll mend,
as we have never spoken.

On days with the strength to only mutter
Got any spare change, brother?
I speak to the wingtips, the pumps and the loafers.
on and on you march so close to the gutter.

(continued on next page)

I am your father,

I am your son,

Care for me for I am you.

Love me for I am.

WES JAMISON

A Silent Tear Falls

Like a familiar stranger
the night embraces me
shrouding my soul in darkness
forcing me to face the emptiness
confronting me with my lonliness
drowning me in despair
crushing me under the weight of nothingness

I accept my lover's embrace
fully aware of my yearnings
knowing another night has come
wondering if another dawn awaits
will I survive this night
as I have so many others
will this night prove too much

Like so many mornings before
I will wake up alone
the arms of the night lost
to the warming rays of the sun
leaving me naked, lost, and alone
fully exposed to the world
vulnerable and frightened

(continued on next page)

I curl up in a fetal position
embracing my own body
as no one else seems willing
hugging my knees to my chest
clutching what's left of my soul
staring at the pieces of my broken heart
laid bare on the ground in front of me

a silent tear falls

WES JAMISON

Once Again, Alone

the darkness draws closer
as I face another lonely night
with only a pillow to hold

my arms reach for a person
i grasp hold of nothingness
the knot in my throat tightens

tears stream down my face
my chest aches within me
my mind races, searching

is there nothing more for me
will this aching emptiness
last forever and for eternity

are we not made for each other
were we not given to each other
by One who reaches out for us

darkness and light mingle
is it a trick of the tears and light
or is there a Presence here

(continued on next page)

does my loneliness know an end
does One walk with me in the darkness
or are shadows my only companions

the clock ticks on my wrist
without the gentle, constant clicking
the sound of silence would overpower

slowly the loneliness wears me down
my racing mind slows to a crawl
sleep comes and I embrace the night

once again, alone

JEFFERY JOHNSON

Breaking The Cycle

I utter a prayer with a weary voice.
The words hit the wall and melt in the shadows.
I raise my eyes and consider my choice.

A rich man in a three-piece suit drives his Rolls Royce
While the poor man in rags shivers and starves in the night.
I utter a prayer with a weary voice.

A girl is taunted by the popular boys.
They call her fat, ugly and loser.
I raise my eyes and consider my choice.

A child awakens to the terrible noise
Of gang members shouting and shooting each other.
I utter a prayer with a weary voice.

A preacher waves a sign shouting in a loud voice
That God hates gays and they are going to hell.
I raise my eyes and consider my choice.

I long for the death of injustice. I long to rejoice.
We can decide to live hatred or to fight it.
I utter a prayer with a weary voice.
I raise my eyes and consider my choice.

HENRY JUHALA

Lamentation For A Grounded Eagle

He was a tender life
Broken by ministry's seductive art
Having walked that path before
Endeared him to my heart

Reconciled to selfless purpose
Redeeming years he lived in vain
But his life the church had strangled
Never soaring as high again

Though the healing of each morning
Gave him vigor to face the day
It was annulled in lamentation
Mourning the fact that he was gay

His trust in Pray TV propaganda
Wouldn't allow for understanding his pain
So another newborn promise
Never soared as high again

He curled up each night all alone
Trapped in a different kind of snare
Stricken by Falwell fundamentalism
Bound by charismaticized despair

(continued on next page)

To deviate from Holiness roots
He thought would indict Christ's reign
So this master of newfound church games
Never soared as high again

His innocent joy of youth
Graced with accents of love
Bowed to learned suffering and torment
Escaping the peace of the dove

Once a treasure, fertile with hope
Now compromised the blood that was slain
To be secure and above reproach
Never soared as high again

Substituting visible form for grace
Inherent in erroneous prison wall
So crippled by no design of his own
Here the church must take the fall

Like an eagle whose broken wing
Was put in a splint to heal the pain
Until the splint could be removed
Never soared as high again

What was meant to be a bandage
Became bondage away from flight
And until totally unfastened
Never soared into the night

(continued on next page)

In mutual unspoken covenant

His talents forced to constrain

Confined to long ago forgotten splint

Never soared as high again

HENRY JUHALA

Sweet Memories Are All I Have

Since I have nothing else of his at all
I recall the objects we shared before
Posters of idols that hung on the wall
Church choir, romantic movies, the door
And key which carried me to him awhile
The quiet retreats, favorite restaurants and the sand
We raised in walks along the beach, the smile
And gleam in his eyes only I could understand

When I survey our past together
All earth's treasures cannot take his place
Nor can heaven's cherubim
And only now I see how much he gave me
Heaven and earth, and every tie I have to him
So I relish each thought, whether sad or cheery
Since little else remains
But sweet memory.

HENRY JUHALA

...And That's The Way It Was

Listen to what I have to say
I can't hide in the closet anymore
Former child of peaceful night and simple day
That's the way it was when I was four

Pentecostals separated from the world
In the Bible belt where everything was straight
Went to Sunday School where life's secrets were unfurled
That's the way it was when I was eight

Between memorizing Bible verses
And uncovering riddles entombed on library shelves
I began rising above social and economic curses
That's the way it was when I was twelve

Self-assured and full of confidence
Yet dreaming far away of Malibu and Liechtenstein
I still couldn't ask a girl to a dance
Even though I was finally sweet sixteen

Engrossed in work, school and church, a social life to mourn
Young professional to pay for college bills aplenty
Judeo-Christian ethic by now slightly worn
That's the way it was when I turned twenty

(continued on next page)

No longer blind to hand-me-down theology
Got my own place. Freedom knocking at my door
Finally expressing love, not with her, but with he
That's the way it was when I turned twenty-four

Except for hiding from sister and brother
No longer afraid to take him on a date
Without guilt I can embrace a lover
That's the way it was when I was twenty-eight

The church is finally reaching all people
God's blessings have been poured out anew
Straights and gays under one steeple
A pleasant surprise when I turned thirty-two

The more I come out to members of my family
The more of me they think someone should fix
A few understand it's how God made me
It's more than just a phase, considering I'm thirty-six

God has given me a partner, someone I truly adore
Armando is best thing to happen to me
Now at last I have someone to live life for
I'm abundantly blessed and full of life, finally at forty

I grieve Armando's passing. Wonder how life can go on
Gay Christian friends become my family
They're the only ones I can truly rely on
Now that I am an old man of forty-four

(continued on next page)

Moved to a city far away from everything I know that's gay

Got a new car, new house, new job, no spouse

Cornfields bring me full circle to my Dakota roots

I feel like a kid again, now that I'm a young man of forty-eight

ERIK J. KOEPNICK

Revelation On Admiration

For once no words are had by me,
To ascertain my sanity;
For once I thought no one might be,
But found, have I, a charming he.

MARK KOERBER

The Poor Are Everywhere

The poor are everywhere
on the corner, man and woman
greasy-headed,
his ears full of hearing aids,
she grunting
"unh, unh, unh"
and pushing the air around
with twisted hands.
I do not speak her language
neither does her man.

The old, frail wasted person
in the wheelchair
(so old, so wasted
I cannot tell gender
and certainly cannot stare)
whirrs past.

And that guy, wild red hair
hunched on the curb
in front of the Starbucks
two-fisting
a floury bun
gnawing it's white flesh

(continued on next page)

with violent tiny grinding bites.

He carefully examines each post-bite reduction

of his only bread

staring as if some other mouth

steals his nourishment

each time he turns

to mutter secrets into the air.

And the guy

in the Drew Bledsoe jersey

looking like a bath house derelict

wandering the Castro

in '74.

Wild-eyed from huffing

all night long

bent over in a dark room

huffed beyond pain or pleasure.

The poor are everywhere

always with us, not happy peasants

singing earthy ditties

and dancing circles

in praise of sun and moon and harvest.

Not hardy workers

laboring for freedom

in clouds of gas,

burying those who have passed

through iron doors into liberation.

(continued on next page)

And not some higher-educated
yippie, hippie, funky-dreaded
granola munching prophets of the "simple life"
eschewing the comfort of civil society
to demonstrate to us
our quiet desperation.

The poor are everywhere among us
the stooped woman with a shopping cart
loaded, overflowing with plastic shopping bags.
The tall old man
with the aristocratic bearing
standing on the corner, violin in hand,
mumbling to each passerby
"how about a little Mozart."
He pushes a few bars from the strings
hurried, pressured, and soft
like his speech.
We throw coins into his violin case.
At least he offered something.

The poor are everywhere
will always be with us
following us
coloring the way
to breakfast out
always with us.

And as we nibble ten dollars eggs
and sip fair-trade coffee (continued on next page)

and congratulate ourselves

that an Ecuadorian peasant

still lives his traditional lifestyle

and tip the college-boy waiter

more than 20% because we remember our

days of waiting tables for beer money,

the guy with the wild red hair

shoves his uneaten bun

deep into his pocket

and shouts his way into

the traffic waiting for the light to change to green.

JOSE A. LOPEZ "JOALBY"

Everyone Is White

Everyone is White.
Devoid. Lacking. Wanting.
Craving.
Suppressing.
A Blank Canvas waiting to have someone else come and paint them into who they think they are supposed to be.
No body. No heart.
No feelings.
No remorse.

Everyone is white.
No color. No sound. No substance.
Empty and vast space.
No mind no thought.
Abandoned and without an image.

Everyone is white.
Not truly who they are but never fully who they are not.
Everyone is white and looking for the place where the color will land in the right places and paint the picture of them and their lives.
Everyone is white.
Never happy where they are.

Everyone is white.
Never where they have to be.

(continued on next page)

Never who they have to be.

Eraser marks covering the backdrop.

Like a shaken Etch-A-Sketch.

Everyone is white.

Everyone has nothing.

Everyone is nothing.

Nobody is anyone.

Nobody is somebody.

Everyone is non-existant.

Everyone is looking to matter, looking to make a difference.

Noone ever truly does.

EVERYONE IS WHITE. AND TODAY I FEEL THE WHITEST.

GREGORY LOSELLE

Magdalene Penitent, After De La Tour

Light flickers in the skull's eye-sockets
from the candle on the table nested
in spilled wax, the old wood thickened
with the tears of other evenings. Crumbs
pock out stars across the grain, half light
half shadow, twitching. She sighs,
presses her finger to her tongue, thinks
of the emptiness behind each object,
grubs up the crumbs across the table,
feeling them crunch.
               They taste of salt
and dried blood, and the dirt under her nails:
like iron and rock and hot, trapped air.
Turning the crumbs on the bed
of her tongue, her mouth becomes
the tomb, dry hot and arched
in empty darkness; she sees again
the filled pyx spilling on the path
where, the crusted cloths cast off,
the garden breaks into bloom
around her, ripe fruit bending down
the boughs, and the gardener, as she sees
him, standing guard beside the open
door.

(continued on next page)

She wets her fingers, snuffs
the candle out. Each incarnation shrugs
the others off. The skull's eye-sockets fill.

TIMOTHY METZNER

Walk-on Role

when you creep in
unannounced
my life slows for a few seconds
blink
stomach tightens
remind myself how to breathe
because i am faced with the glaring truth:

you exist.

you have not evaporated
nor vanished.
all of my efforts to avoid
cannot make you disappear
forever

you always do this
sneak in at moments of least suspect
its been four hours that I haven't thought of you
and in a moment you
materialize

to stiffen my body
and snap open my memory

(continued on next page)

with a numbing buzz that suffocates all other sound

my chest contracts
fight to force back emotion
struggle to not succumb
'this is a ghost
a shadow
a reflection'
i say
not you
not the real you

and it ends

the moment passes
life reboots
with a new unwelcome stamp of you on my skin

stop this.

its easier
when you don't exist
at all

LUCAS MIX

Crucifixion

Your body, hung upon a tree
Sorrows pressed upon your brow
The words of friends
Beat upon you
As a lover's heart slowly fading
You strain to hear the sound of failing breath
The touch of other
The hands you held, the feet you washed
But silent they beat and distant
As you hung upon a tree

A word, hung upon your lips
In that moment unfulfilled
A promise waiting
Beats upon you
What cost that word
Torn from your throat by a lover almost too far gone to hear
The voice of other
Echoed in my head
Tortured me with love
Silent and distant
As you hung upon a tree

A star, hung upon a hook

(continued on next page)

Torn from the heavens by my need
Cast by God, crying, to the ground
As though I ripped his very heart out by my leaving
and I stand there
too aghast to see your tears
Too frightened now at what the leaving cost you
What price, my love,
That left you helpless
Bare before my eyes
In flesh that I distained
As you hung upon a tree

Heaven torn in two
Stars fallen, burning to the Earth
Like flaming death that reaps the souls of men
Shockwaves blast my heart
And leave me, ashen as a shadow on the wall
We find no meaning in Death
Until it finds us
Waiting in the dark

A promise, whispered to the night
Cast by your lips in failing breath
Fell like benediction on my brow
I would not hear the heavens crash about my feet
As stars came burning to the ground
But still
In my foolishness,
I lean close to hear those whispered words

(continued on next page)

As though your death had somehow brought us closer

The world ended on that day
The heavens crashed
The angels came
And I did not see
But in the quiet of the night
You whispered in my ear
That there was more
For you rose again
Brighter than before
And far more deadly

That I should dare to love you rends my soul
Am I strong enough to bear the heat of your gaze?
To see you, dimmed upon the cross was pain enough
But this regard, this gentle look
This love
From one arisen
To love you, gentle as a man, and harmless, that was pain enough
But this power, this glory
Dare I love a God?

What tokens might he ask who died in courting me?
What must I do to show my love
To him who caught the stars and made the whole world new
That I might not escape his love?

Joy, fills me to the brim

(continued on next page)

And this I bring to you, my love

Who died for me

Repentance and release

I bring nothing but acceptance of your gift

To bring my heart to the table

That it might be broken

And offered up

AL-ANTONY MOODY

The Adulteress

He was the Light
He was the Dawn
He was The Son Of God
He was God's First Born

She was the Darkness
She was the Night
She was an Adulteress
She be judged with right

For the beauty of stones wait to kiss her death
For the beauty of her heart Jesus had not left

She stood next to the lepers, the blind and the lame
For The Law of Moses now called her shame

Tears ran down her face as fast as hope left her skin
Jesus drew a line in the sand and asked those who had not sinned
To cast the first stone
To throw the first rock
To those who had not sinned there was not

Not one soul was left to cast a stone
Jesus said, "Sin no more woman… go home"
For Mercy and Kindness upholds his heavenly throne

Judge not me before you cast your rock
Look deep into your heart for love

Inspired by John 8:1-10 & Proverbs 20:28

AL-ANTONY MOODY

Jesus Christ – The Last Kiss

I will write a message of love with my hot-wet tongue across your breast
I will look into the doves of your eyes when I come to rest

You are but the strongest adorning tree
I shelter my naked bosom beneath thee

You are but the sweetest wine that presses hard to my lips
Your body is but a feasting banquet of food that I relish

Like a stag you blaze and buck the night
Like a gazelle I bask in your eternal light

This bed fruitful and spreading like a bountiful grazing flock
Milk and honey dripping in the kiss of myrrh, in the kiss of love

I faint with love and succumb into your arms
You are the dawn, the moon…the stars

I am but a bud waiting to blossom into a dawn of lush flowers
Waiting for your seed to deliver me high into your mounting tower

Even when I sleep my heart satiates with My Lords desire
To taste you again and again, my loving Messiah

The fragrance of perfume spreads with a passionate hunger
Filling the sweet brute air with a sensual passion to humble

You are my salvation…and my loving key
I am your faithful servant latch-opening…deliver into me.

Inspired by *The Bible*, Song of Songs 1:1-8

AL-ANTONY MOODY

"Last Stop!" – Abandoned Train Station

Broken and rundown
A man stood at an abandoned train station
Home bound

Every night he stood there
Through sun, rain, hail and frost
Waiting for the train to stop

To be given passage
To be let on
Why was he out there?
Maybe we will never know…

Was he homeless?
Was he poor?
Stuck in a dream
Of wanting to dream forever more

Through the years my eyes met his
Enraptured like a kiss
A tear fell from it
Falling onto broken-cracked pavement
Giving life to grass and flowers all around it

Other passengers on the train frowned
And looked away…
Pretending not to notice him every day

Some smiled
Some blew kisses
Some only got glimpses

Some spoke about all the things they'd bought in town

(continued on next page)

Trying not to notice the man at the abandoned train stop
Where all the factories had closed down
Where industry one day just slowed and stopped
Where everything was lost

The buildings were crumbling
The factories empty like hearts that had never known love
Wasting into the sear of dust

I looked for the man every night
Especially tonight
Sadness had gripped my very soul
Through the years as suffering unfolds
I just wished to God the train would stop
To let this man on, just once

The train slowly came to the abandoned train station stop
For the first time allowing the man to get on
People cheered, smiled and cried
For their sins Jesus Christ had died

The doors opened
Light poured in, engulfing the train
Filling it with an overpowering of love
Some people fainted, some succumbed into his arms

Falling to our knees
We fell like the breaking of waves on rocks
We were now found
Not abandoned or lost
The speaker sang joyfully, "Last stop!"

CONNIE SCHROEDER

Beauty…Divine Feminine

My desire is to walk her paths
bathe in her oceans
rest on her strong comforting breasts
as I wander the mountains
feel the touch of her embrace
  on a warm breezy day
taste her sweet honeycomb,
  plump, juicy apples and golden corn.
Let me smell her hot blackberries in the sun,
freshly baked bread
  my favorite soup simmering on the stove
or the delicate scent of lavender.

I want to see her many shapes, sizes and colors…
  in the old woman crone whose face crumples
    into a million wrinkles as she smiles;
  in the child who sings a made up rhyme,
    and dances through the garden,
  in the mother who holds a newborn baby,
    feeding the child from her own warm,
        soft mother body, sleepily at 3:00 am.
I want to be aware of the life force,
moving
  in every stone or tree
      child, brother, sister,
            poet, singer, weaver, dancer,
  giant redwood tree, spawning salmon
        dancing ash tree, spider and web; silent moment;
            leaf and blade of grass

First love of my soul
  May I learn of faithfulness from you…

(continued on next page)

offering yourself for your beloved
giving your body to a million lovers longing for your kiss,
nurturing our souls with tenderness
   with grace, with wisdom.

CONNIE SCHROEDER

A New Name

The night is dark
My spine tingles
As the dog and I make our way across the yard
Under the apple trees
Whose branches catch at my clothing
Where the darkness seems most complete
And my heart catches in my throat
As I expect a stranger to step out of the shadows
And wrestle me to the ground.

I have been wrestling
Through the darkness God
Wanting simple answers
Where there are none
Wanting easy happiness
When you are asking me to grasp hope
Wanting pain to ease
When I know, my life will never be the same.

I have been wrestling
Through a long, dark night
Asking a blessing
Unwilling, to let you go,
Unwilling, to accept no,
For an answer. (continued on next page)

You gave Jacob, the usurper a new name
One who wrestled
With humans and with God
And who prevailed.
A name that acknowledged his weakness
As his power.

Have you a new name for the thief?
The gossip? The liar? The lost?
Have you a new name for the murderer?
The despicable, crafty one who waits for her chance?
Have you a new name for the adulterer?
The prostitute?
The one who beats his spouse?
The one who cheats on the algebra test
And the one who is addicted
To drugs, to alcohol, to sex, to work?
What about a name for the one
who doesn't fit in the family?

Do you have new names for us God?

We are here, your people
Asking a blessing of you
Asking here in the shadows
Looking for you in the stranger
With whom we struggle
Listening for your voice

(continued on next page)

For the name which is ours

The name you have spoken

The truth you know

That we have yet to discover

In ourselves.

The night is dark here,

There is no stranger in the shadows,

And the branches grasping at me are only branches

But I linger a moment,

No promises of descendents and a billion stars

Only a blessing in the darkness

By One Mysterious

Who speaks a name

Which only I can hear

And know to be my own.

CONNIE SCHROEDER

Practicing Presence

Another day of living
Early morning dog walk
On frosted grassy fields
Canine friends cavorting
Happily, snuffling
through the leaves, running free
Playfully chasing each other

Margaret and I hold hands
Wordless
I think about love
That holds us
Walks with us
Guides us
She thinks about the screen door
And that her routine got interrupted
This morning
So her coffee won't be
Waiting when we return
To the warm house

I used to think my thoughts
Higher somehow
Than her practicality.

(continued on next page)

But now it runs

Together and I know

It's all just God

In different guises

Like some prankster

Hiding behind the coffee pot

She jumps out

And says "Surprise!"

"You serious poet…Get real

The dog needs a bath

And checks need to be written.

Practice my presence

In the details

You marvelous mystic

Make a pot of soup

water the geranium

And look for me there

Beneath the leaves

Cavorting and snuffling

Bubbling away…"

CONNIE SCHROEDER

Bent Over Woman

In my mind's eye I see you
Bent over, nearly bent double
Walking into the synagogue that day

Jesus saw you.
What was it like to be seen by him?
He called you to him.

My heart leaps to think
What that might have been like
To have been singled out...
to have been seen
to have him calling my name.

Did you know of him?
Were you wanting to disappear back
into the crowd again?

Or did you go to him, knowing the kindom was near?
Did you know the miracle would happen
Or did it take you by surprise?

So you came to him
you, who were bent over, double

(continued on next page)

looking always at the earth beneath your feet,
or perhaps turning your head sideways to see
found yourself looking right into his eyes
because knowing Jesus,
knowing just the way he is,
he got on his knees to speak to you

He simply told you that you were free…
And you found yourself standing straight
And tall
Still looking into his eyes
then gazing around yourself in wonder.

What was it like?
Was there an explosion of light and joy
Within your body?

Or was it simply
That Jesus spoke peace
To the tension and the pain
And it flowed away
Like the Jordan
Flowing on?

Bent Over Woman
I would like to know your name
To hear you tell the story
Of the miracle
To experience the song of praise in your voice
To see the joy dancing in your eyes (continued on next page)

I smile

For as I look in the mirror

I see you there in me

Smiling a crooked smile

Your back straight and strong

Daughter of God

Set free

And beloved.

RICHARD TETREAULT

When

Is it right to marshal in
the absurdities in life
and agree with their recognitions
where substance cries out
To be heard
and love cries out
for support?
Who told you your prejudices
were just
and your hatreds could bloom
like flowers
in a forest of crippling
wing bites
where birds are forced
not to fly?

RICHARD TETREAULT

This Is My Love

Is my love that compelling
that I must seek its happening pause;
undressed in a new place though old
impressed by a secular cause.
Imprisoned for years within a
scurrilous mantra
bowed by the world of its undulant magic;
oftener have I thought of God in a hurry
when seldom should I have thought
of things unimagined.
What is real is not necessarily true for you
as hope should be alive in every mind;
what was once better is now blatantly worse,
empowered by something not easily told.
If God is truth what then are your lies
and is faith only concerned with what
is disturbing?
Time is the aspect inherently prized
that patience awaits from its standing.
And what of your infallibility
which possesses the word of God:
if yours is the only true word,
then behave as though it were.
Love's expressions are always divine

(continued on next page)

greater than words and music combined:

it is God's great bestowal legitimately worn

for which it has sought to reside.

I rail against words abused by your power

in judgments you make against my humanity:

am I not a creature of God's as well

standing oppressed in the heart of your hell?

Do I stand to be graced by a Jesuitical

awakening

that slowly takes leave of my childhood

horrors

countering thoughts that menace my awareness

of being who I was as God's young imposter.

I reject your concept of Christ's mission

that exists just beneath your false toothed

smile.

Your denial of my face

is not only sin.

it is dogma prevailing

over God's forgiving.

I may not know your vision's delights

and neither do you know mine;

what I now know best is the love

I possess

Whose light will live with me

to my last breath;

for God made my heart to stir

your unrest

as you've loudly condemned

love between men.

RICHARD TETREAULT

Untitled

A victorious sunset
cools past my door
as I awaken
sadly from the shore
where sex and religion
placed a hex on the new pope
who delights in spying
and accuses me of lying
when all I have done
is admit that I am gay.
Who told him I was vulnerable
enough to shout obscenities
at the least of my brethren
in exchange for a half baked confession
dedicated to the late John Paul the Second
and to the homophobia that exists in Poland
long enough to astound
the lesser of the two Swiss guards
standing on the corner
of Hollywood and Vine?

ROBERT THOMPSON

Ballad Of Billy's Body

For the last time Billy said
his "goodbyes" before leaving.
He hated saying goodbye.
He preferred going away
before anyone noticed
being far away when they did.

Saying goodbye makes one's
departure seem more important
than is, Billy thought.
Tears make it harder to leave.
One always feels guilty about
leaving as if somehow
it weren't natural never joyous
about larger worlds still to
explore and to pass beyond.

1. Billy's Mind

Saying goodbye makes it sound
so final. For Billy, nothing was
ever final. He was forever throwing
things away--photographs, teapots--
or giving things away. Objects tie

(continued on next page)

one down, inhibit freedom of movement,
Billy always said. But in his mind
Billy never turned loose of anyone.
Briefest affections were never
forgotten, no matter how long ago.
In Billy's mind the silent conversation
of kisses and senseless words continued,
the elaboration endless.

2. Billy's Body

The world was treacherous.
Nothing ever stayed nailed down.
No decisions decisive--
life's agenda would play itself
no matter what.
No angers could last.
Loves arise like the Phoenix
from the ashes of angers forgotten
to fly, to run and even to soar.

But the years pass and the lines
on Billy's face increase.
The Practical Problem of
Billy's Body became overwhelming--
he could not be everywhere at once.

Jerry growing up in Waycross and
Larry's moving into "mid-life" in

(continued on next page)

Anchorage and Mother growing old
in some other world, went right
along as if Billy were not there.

3. Not Dead but Dreaming

Mozart and David Hockney photopaintings.
Another generation of faces on
these old streets. Laughter--
purely joyous and without reference.
Trying to decipher the precise
moment at which these cut pink roses--
full and fragrant--have become
no longer so. "Billy would have
loved it," I smiled to myself,
"But he is not here."

ROBERT THOMPSON

Wireless Imagination

1.

Is when the lines go dead
No messages sent nor received
Prairie winds hang the
lines heavy with ice
All is brittleness
and crystalline light
Arctic winds make the wires hum
hummm Ommm Om Opacity
Strung out across miles and
miles of desolation and waste
from sea to shining sea
The power is out
The lines are down
Dead on the hook
Wires and miles miles after miles
of black taut stretched broken wire
No dial tones
No Morse Code clacking
in the telegraph receivers
Dial Zero
for Operator-Emergency Repairs
Operator-Emergency Repairs
cannot be reached   (continued on next page)

2.

Dial D for Deafness Dumbness
Dereliction Depression
Dysentery Dehydration
Death and Decay
Random dialings on a dead phone
Obscenities exhaled into the night
of numbers numberless as the bright
starts of cloudless summer nights
No transmissions No connexions
We cannot send our regrets
Wireless imagination is when
the lines go dead the power is out
No messages sent nor received
Wireless imagination looks over
your shoulder and plays with
the lights in your mind

3.

Is when all letters
add up to nought
Finest-crafted simple paragraphs
straightforward and clean are not sent
Nimble fingers light and certain
on typewriter keys do not program
There is no printout

(continued on next page)

There is no in-put
There are no erasures
Nothing is lost
Memory is clear
Nothing retrievable
Mouths are open
Hollow vestibules of
voices like the sea
heard in conch shells placed
to our ears on dry land
The roar in our ears
is not the sea

4.

When the last pieces have
been moved on the board
When the house curtains come
down across the stages
When the bed sheets have
been neatly folded
When the photographs
have been put away and
the letters burned
When the books have been
given away and favorite tea
cups given to favorite friends
When the final words have been
spoken and nothing more can be said

(continued on next page)

When the last tears have been shed
and there is no more crying
There is finally sitting down--
palms upturned--in the dust

5.

The gods have come down
We have seen their faces in
total strangers--some of whom
have become our friends for a time
Fire and ice and blistering winds
The sound of an anonymous aluminum
can racing emptily across the pavement

Darkness Wetness Coldness

All the days are short

FRED TURPIN

One Tender Touch

My hand falls heavy on the page,
Body dense, tight with weight
From last night's sleepless night with you.
My eyes refused to close; dreams stayed away,
When in the night I felt your touch,
Kept awake till dawn from wanting more.

It was enough-one touch;
Enough to know you reached for me.
No words, no eyes, just a sleepy touch,
Intentional in its gift of love.
A moment's contact with your skin,
Turning me to you.

FRED TURPIN

May The Shrine Catch Fire
For Al and Richard

Know that as you endure his love,
As you wake each morning
More fully aware of who he is,
You receive and give a gift.
He came exactly when
You needed him to come
And you came to him
When he was ready.

When you looked deeply
Into his eyes, you saw his being.
He opened, as did you.
The tight shoe slipped off
And the heart softened-fell more
Deeply into him as he fell into you.

Trust the power of love to heal,
Let it seep through every nerve
And into every muscle.
Make love in candlelight,
Rub his body with oil,
See him without shame or fear,
Let every wild desire be expressed.
Let your passion be holy passion.

(continued on next page)

He is not one, but many.
Allow his many flowers to blossom;
Pick not one, but breathe in
Each fragrance; swim to the place
Where there is no constriction,
No safety, no boundary to your love.

Be so deeply with him,
That when he moans, you hear
The sound of your own voice.
When you touch his inner thigh,
You touch yourself.
Breathe him in, as though
He is the breath of your being,
The source of your hope,
The grace of your healing.

FRED TURPIN

Insisting On My Nakedness

Once, while lying in bed,
His hands caressing my back
With a tenderness my body
Had never known,
I realized I'd longed for this,
Unconsciously searched, yearned
My way from man to man,
Looking to be held
In a way that would feel "forever."

Then again, it wasn't once
Nor was it twice or three times
But a repetition of his loving-kindness,
Like balm upon my back, my arms,
My thighs…Insisting on my nakedness,
His touch a touch that does not lie,
That in some strange manner
More believable than words,
Seeps between defenses of my mind,
Soaks into the pores of my skin
And into bones that hold no memory
Of being held in love the way he loves.

My body is not some grave
That receives a lifeless body.

(continued on next page)

It is a living thing that breathes
As it takes in, receives, envelopes
What is slowly placed inside,
Shouldering the heavy weight
As though it were as light as the soul.
Bodily, it responds
With sighs of gratitude,
Moans of pleasure,
And a deeper desire to give in return,
To honor, love the giver who
Breathes beside, reciprocates,
Dreams together one dream.

FRED TURPIN

Loving His Company
For Jeff

Again, our paths crossed.
He standing there with a smile
Of recognition that lasted through
Three cigarettes, two glasses of wine
And the drive to his apartment and bed.

He said he enjoyed my company
And I enjoyed every inch of him,
Even more his warm heart-
Large and round and roomy,
Filled with sweetness.
This man adds new definition
To goodness of heart.

In the middle of the night, he turned
And we were face to face,
Our foreheads touched in sleep.
I felt his breath soft across my face,
Like the tender Breath of God---
Made me aware how connected are
Love and life, sex and energy
As I breathed in his scent,
His soccer legs strong
As they moored against my thigh.

And in my dream,
A stranger walked up to my old car,
Raised the hood and poured
Coolant into the radiator.
So obvious, it made me smile
The same smile I saw on his face,
Loving his company.

Made in United States
Orlando, FL
28 July 2022

20294078R00078